A circular outdoor cistern at Poundisford Park, S⋯ ⋯ain spectacular (1671).

DECORATIVE LEADWORK

P. M. Sutton-Goold

Shire Publications Ltd

CONTENTS

Printed in Great Britain by C. I. Thomas & Sons (Haverfordwest) Ltd, Press Buildings, Merlins Bridge, Haverfordwest, Dyfed SA61 1XF.

British Library Cataloguing in Publication Data: Sutton-Goold, P. M. Decorative leadwork. 1. Decorative leadwork, history. I. Title. 739. 54. ISBN 0-7478-0082-0.

ACKNOWLEDGEMENTS
Illustrations are acknowledged as follows: University of Cambridge, pages 3, 9, 13, 15 (centre); The British Museum, pages 7, 14, 16 (top); Sotheby's, page 6; Suffolk County Council, pages 4, 5, 8 (bottom), 15 (top and bottom), 18 (bottom left), 29 (bottom); Jarrolds Colour Publications, page 8 (top left); Anglia Roof Company, Norwich, page 10; H. M. Colvin, pages 8 (top right), 25 (bottom right); Victoria and Albert Museum, page 16 (centre); Colchester and Essex Museum, page 17 (top); Eastern Counties Newspapers Limited, page 21 (left); The Royal Commission on Historical Monuments, pages 21 (right), 23, 26; The National Trust, pages 19, 22, 24, 30; Oxford University, page 25 (top left and right); Museum of London, page 29 (top); St Fagans Museum, page 28; Country Life, page 1. Trust for Lincolnshire Archaeology (drawing by Cecily Marshall), page 2; Jonathan Gaunt, cover.

Cover: *A decorated leaden cistern at Neston Park, Corsham, Wiltshire, the home of Sir John and Lady Fuller.*

A restored Roman tank found in a well at Ashton, Northamptonshire, 15 inches (380 mm) deep by 34 inches (860 mm) wide. It had been used to block the well, which contained pottery and coins from the late fourth century AD, so it may predate these.

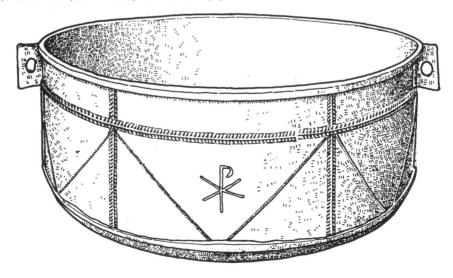

This Roman tank was found in good condition in a field at Burwell, Cambridgeshire, in 1977, near some pottery of the fourth century AD, the presumed date of the tank. It has a capacity of 45 gallons (205 litres), being roughly 25½ inches (650 mm) in diameter and 17½ inches (440 mm) in depth.

LEADWORK IN THE ANCIENT WORLD

Lead was the first metal to be smelted from ore as it was naturally available in the region between south-east Turkey and the southern tip of the Caspian Sea, near to where civilisation is thought to have originated. The smelting process began before 4000 BC. One of the earliest known leaden objects, dated to 3800 BC, is a female figurine from the Temple of Osiris at Abydos in Upper Egypt. 2 inches (50 mm) tall, it is beautifully tooled and sculpted from a lump of smelted, hardened lead. The facial characteristics appear to have been incised with sharp tools and a gouge.

Two or three centuries later writing developed in Mesopotamia, in the world's first known cities. An alphabet of 'cuneiform' (wedge-shaped) lettering was used and examples on clay or metal tablets and memorials have survived. When handwriting developed, sheet lead was manufactured, sometimes simply by being pressed between two flat stones, and lettering could be scored on to the surface with a simple stylus.

Evidence suggests that open moulds were widely used for making small artefacts in the Near East during the fourth millennium BC. In about 2800 BC a technological breakthrough, the 'lost wax' casting method, increased the scope of the lead caster, who could then manufacture rounded forms for the imaginative or realistic portrayal of human or divine figures. Recognisable details of plants and animals could now be reproduced and laborious finishing processes were unnecessary. In about 2500 BC solid-cast leaden figures began to be superseded when hollow-core casting was invented in the Near East, greatly reducing the quantity of lead required for each object.

A Roman tank, which contained a mass of iron objects and fragments of smelted-down lead when discovered at Icklingham, Suffolk. It measures 35 inches (890 mm) in diameter and is 14½ inches (370 mm) deep.

From the eastern Mediterranean the Phoenicians built up an international trade in tin ingots, tin being a necessary ingredient of solder, and the practice of lead casting became commonplace in the region that is now Iran, Iraq and Syria. Separately cast parts could be joined by soldering. Many examples of ancient hollow figures, sometimes less than 1 inch (25 mm) high or long, representing birds, camels, elephants, mounted horsemen or charioteers, from Egypt and other parts of the Near East have been preserved in museum collections. Tooled, sometimes gilded rings, brooches and pins for personal or commercial use, toys, votive objects for religious rites and small tools for the goldsmith required only small quantities of lead, which had the advantage that it could easily be reused by being recast and reshaped. Simple portable foot bellows gave the operators the freedom to create intricate shapes and to apply designs inspired by their environment.

As the ancient Greeks developed their trade throughout the Aegean region, lead seems to have continued to be used for small objects for private, domestic or religious purposes. As cult worship changed continuously, lead was very suitable for casting new or changed votive offerings.

By the eighth century BC leaden weights, sometimes shaped like animals, were being used by Assyrian traders, and later by Greeks and Romans. Anchors were partially leaden and leaden spindle whorls were widely distributed throughout the civilised world.

Surviving small leaden objects of Roman origin include candle-holders, small bowls like large teacups, and girdle hangers which resembled the medieval chatelaine and were used for carrying personal possessions. Roman leaden seals, generally used as military, imperial or private marks, often for labelling consignments of goods, continue to be discovered during excavations in England and Wales.

One of the smallest but most widely used items of exchange in the Roman Empire until the third century AD was the *tessera*, a small leaden block or token. Categorised and identified by simple symbols or inscriptions, tesserae replaced silver coin on several occasions when the expense of maintaining armies had induced inflation. *Frumentariae*, tesserae bearing a wheat-ear motif, were exchanged for food. *Spectae* were tesserae that served as admission tickets to the arena or theatre. Their validity was gradually extended to include admission to public baths, to specific groups or societies, and for use as boat tickets for voyages abroad.

Roman votive plaques of lead compound have been found, often with inscriptions in incised dots, such as 'To the god Silvanus the coppersmith gladly pays his vow'. Leaden ingots found on Roman sites in Britain bear stamped inscriptions indicating their origins to have been Derbyshire, Clwyd, Yorkshire and the Mendips.

It is uncertain when lead was first used for storage tanks. Underground water supplies for cities in the ancient Middle East could be conserved in bedrock or in stone troughs at various levels; sometimes clay containers were used. But in about 550 BC when the Babylonian king Nebuchadnezzar wished to please his wife Amythis he created the fabulous Hanging Gardens of Babylon with a sophisticated built-in irrigation system. Giant arches of rock supported large troughs made from soldered sheets of lead in which aromatic plants and fruits were grown. Several centuries later the Romans introduced ambitious water-supply systems in parts of their empire using large quantities of pipes made from sheet lead. The cast sheets were cut, then hammered or bent round solid-core mandrels or moulds, and finally fused in the round by a flow of molten lead poured along the seam which faced downwards in the sand of the mould.

In ancient Rome tanks were constructed from lead sheets cast in a frame of sand which was sometimes moulded with herring-bone or line patterns formed by marking the sand with small objects or block dies before casting. Bent or hammered into rounded or rectangular containers, the sheets were soldered at the seam and to the base.

More than twenty Roman leaden tanks have been recovered in Britain, some bearing inscriptions, string designs and/or the 'chi-rho' symbol. Frequently oval or circular in plan, some have attached lugs (ears), which perhaps provided leverage or suspension points for carrying to where they were installed to store water, grain or other items. The Ashton tank was found near the river Nene in Northamptonshire on the site of a former Roman town where evidence for ironworking hearths had been found. The tank has a chi-rho monogram formed from three strips of lead 5½ inches (140 mm)

long. Another tank was found at Icklingham, Suffolk, in 1971. Some of the chi-rho tanks are thought to have been used for purification or baptismal rites by Christians in Britain, France and Germany during the second, third and perhaps fourth centuries AD.

In 1988 a leaden panel patterned with saltires and a chi-rho symbol was discovered in a fourth-century Roman well shaft at Caversham, Berkshire. Now in Reading Museum and reconstructed as a font, it is 24 inches (610 mm) deep and 32 inches (810 mm) in diameter. It may predate the well by perhaps a century.

More than two hundred Roman coffins have been found in Britain, some large enough for two or three bodies. They are made from sheet lead with moulded designs. Ossuaries, decorated Roman cremation urns averaging 13½ inches (340 mm) in height and 34 inches (860 mm) in circumference, had removable lids and were usually made of moulded leaden sheets with encircling decorative bands of floral motifs.

A close-up of part of the tank from Icklingham, showing a section of the herring-bone bands encircling the tank and the chi-rho symbol, (the first two letters of Christ's name in Greek) which may have signified Christian ownership.

A leaden 'fire-dragon' found in France, auctioned in London in 1988. A type of garden 'conceit' for summer masques, it dates possibly from the early seventeenth century. Smoke is emitted from the mouth and ears.

LEADWORK FROM THE MIDDLE AGES TO THE PRESENT

Lead continued to be used in some parts of Europe after the collapse of the Roman empire, for example in southern Spain and France, though perhaps not widely in England. In AD 532 the Byzantine emperor Justinian embellished the great city of Constantinople (Istanbul) with immense domed palaces and churches, including St Sophia's cathedral. Sheet lead was an ideal material for covering the irregular shapes of the domed rooftops in which reliquaries were installed.

In Britain in about AD 650 the church at Lindisfarne, Northumberland, was repaired with some 'new leadwork' in place of the existing 'Scottish thatch'. Lead was still valued as a cladding material for monastic buildings, especially where it was plentiful, as in Durham, Derbyshire and Yorkshire. The stonework of some Norman castles such as those at Dover and London was capped decoratively with sheet lead. From the fourteenth century towers and turrets in England and Scotland were clad with lead. Rec-

ords for 1402 mention the supply of fresh lead to make '2 cloth' for a trap-door and tower at the Tower of London. Scottish castles maintained their characteristically 'tiled' leaden roofs until the nineteenth century. Narrow sheet lead is still manufactured for leaden organ reeds, using fabric as the surface onto which the molten lead is poured.

In France fifteenth-century roof-tops, in particular that of the Hôtel-Dieu at Beaune, Côte d'Or, scintillated with filigree leadwork on ridges, crockets, finials and statues. These were imitated elsewhere in Europe during the next century.

After the Dissolution of the Monasteries in England in 1539, much lead became available for reuse on secular buildings and for ornamental urns, fountains, cisterns and statues. Ornamental shelf and chimney friezes, 'antiques' for ceilings, candelabra, parcloses (screens) and coats of arms executed in lead were prestigious acquisitions in Tudor England, as were garden conceits.

The roof of the Hôtel-Dieu, Beaune, Côte d'Or, France, built in 1450 with leaden finials or crockets of lace-like design and small figures resembling oriental-style dragons. When painted or gilded, they were clearly visible to approaching travellers. The ingredients for the patina worked on to the leadwork included a by-product of the local wine industry. The coloured roof tiles contrasted dramatically with the curled, gilded leadwork.

On 24th November 1588 the Worshipful Company of Plumbers in London received its foundation charter from Queen Elizabeth I and London became an important centre for plumbing and allied crafts.

Towards the end of the seventeenth century cheaper 'milled' lead, rolled into uniformly even, paper-thin sheets was available for decorative beaten leadwork. There was also a new moulding device which cast and fused lengths of small-diameter pipes, making grand-scale fountain installations possible. Leaden garden furniture carried designs of fruit and flowers based on botanical illustrations.

Much early leadwork was painted or gilded, the statues at Versailles being among the best known examples. Oil gilding of such features as dates, crests and owners' initials on leaden gutter rainheads or cisterns was popular in England from the seventeenth century. The Masters of the Worshipful Company of Painter-Stainers provided guidelines ('Inventions, copies, patterns and draughts') for painters of pennants, banners, coats of arms or crests on a variety of materials, including leadwork and cisterns. The Royal Ordnance Board at Woolwich employed Mrs Jane Hill as their official paintress to paint eighteen water cisterns for the 'stacks of the Pipes there' in 1717. Ten were gilded with the King's initials, GR, and year. Mrs Hill's bill totalled £157 3s ½d. The price of a new cistern was £5.

An early process of enhancement and protection for leadwork became known as 'tinning'. A sheet of tin foil was laid over a sheet of heated lead, causing the tin to melt into the lead. The surface would subsequently be rubbed with resin. Alternatively, and especially when fashioning rainheads, defined areas on a cut-off section of sheet lead could be tinned decoratively by stencilling a design over a previously applied layer of lampblack. Solder tin was applied over the exposed areas of the design with the appropriate copper-headed soldering iron and then coloured if desired. If tinning was applied to leadwork *in situ*, an angled 'scraper head' was needed. Surfaces thus treated required a 'keying' agent to accept the tinning. Immediate patina effects were and still are achieved by producing chemical changes of infinite variety, using a workshop recipe.

Lead may be applied decoratively to the angles of eaves on thatched or leaden roofs. A combination of thatch and lead provided a check to driving rain and to the entry of rats, which were deterred by sharp reed ends. Medieval church roofs were adorned with leaden crests, figures of saints or weather vanes, some of which

Above: *A painted roundel in a mullioned window at Holy Trinity church, Long Melford, Suffolk. Only three rabbits' ears can be seen, the design being symbolic of the Holy Trinity.*

Right: *A startling royal tribute in lead with Charles I's initials, crown and coat of arms adorning St John's College, Oxford. It was commissioned by Archbishop Laud and recorded by the college bursar in 1635.*

Below: *A panel of an outdoor cistern adorned with a design of fruit and flowers set into a frame with surrounding ribbons and a masked drainage point.*

Left: *A forge illustrated in Félibien's handbook on architecture, published in Paris in 1690. C and D are pipe moulds; G is a trimming stove; T is a rasp to prepare joins for soldering with Y and Z.*

Right: *The forge pit (A) was heated with charcoal to smelt lead for ladling into D for casting into sheets on B after the removal of dross. The thickness of the lead sheet was regulated by the strickle (G), which could be raised on the side 'sharps' or rails with wedges of hat felt. Narrow sheets were made on K, with liquid lead poured through L over thick fabric, not over sand. Wooden mandrels (H) provided cylindrical shapes for pipe making. A metal brazier filled with charcoal (I) was inserted into a rolled sheet of lead to heat the seams when being soldered.*

contained reliquaries to invoke the protection of their saintly patrons.

Prepared lead sheets for the roof statues were hammered over wooden models. To avoid corrosion of the roof figures through the formation of acids, the leadwork was soldered together in sections and frequently assembled over a metal rather than a wooden internal framework. Roof finials and pinnacles could also be constructed in this way but they were fastened with hidden hooks on to seams so that sections could be removed for repairs. Birds, especially crows, were liable to damage Gothic roofwork. Slate roofs or tiles gradually replaced lead for new buildings with the spread of industrialisation in nineteenth-century England. William Morris and Sir Edward Burne-Jones began a revival of handcrafts and amongst their work was the design of leadwork for windows. Influenced by Dante Gabriel Rossetti, the painter-poet, their designs drew inspiration from Renaissance and medieval Italy. By the beginning of the twentieth century the Arts and Crafts movement had exponents in the United States and in Europe, including Holland, and the cities of Europe acquired solid, impressive architecture, often with appropriately designed leadwork.

LEADWORKING TODAY

The use of sheet lead has continued in England, modern technology speeding its manufacture and standardising the quality of the product. The standard

9

A 1980s workshop showing freshly made, cooled sheet lead in the sand bed whilst a man operates the strickle bar, nowadays used only to trim the outside edges of the sheet and to score it longitudinally, with cutting teeth attached to the lower edge of the bar.

moistened sand-bed is still prepared by smoothing it flat with hand-held copper planes. Two operators regulate the 'strike', which is machine-aided to produce sheets several times longer and wider than those produced by Roman or medieval craftsmen. Wafer-thin sheets are still obtained by 'milling' or passing the lead between rollers and are sometimes used on modern multi-faceted roof shapes. When cool, the sheets are cut longitudinally, the machine operator guiding a horizontal bar which is fixed to a downward-thrusting knife down the centre of the casting frame. Sold by weight and in rolls, lead sheets bear numbered codes signifying their suitability for decorative or plain leadwork. Sheet lead in narrow widths is still cast on fabric for the manufacture of organ reeds.

Lead casting in sheets or die moulds is done mainly in small workshops. The lead workers frequently carve their own moulds for casting flat, solid or hollow artefacts. Ornamental figurines, finials, garden ornaments and miniature models of fictional characters cast in lead enjoy considerable popularity. Weighted leaden balances marked with a logo are applied to car wheels to act as stabilisers. Leicester is an important centre for lead manufacture, and the Worshipful Company of Plumbers in London continues as an educational and advisory body concerned with all aspects of leadworking, both practical and aesthetic. The Lead Development Association provides data and guidance for users of the metal from its London office.

Craftsmen continue to travel throughout England using portable forges and

Restoration work in 1987 on 'beaten' quatrefoil design leaden panels on lead-clad parapets and roof valleys on the Victorian Gothic St John's Roman Catholic Cathedral, Norwich.

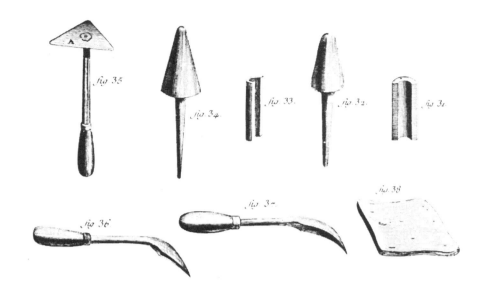

Above and below: *Leadworking tools and equipment: replaceable handles and soldering irons (numbers 31-4); 'rifflers' to reach crevices (36 and 37); solder-stand or drip-plate (38); perforated metal braziers of different lengths to slide into pipes when soldering seams (39 and 40); cutter (41); hook knife for fettling (42); rasp, gouge, chisel and bossing tool (43-6) for treating and shaping lead. (From Diderot's 'Encyclopaedia', 1720.)*

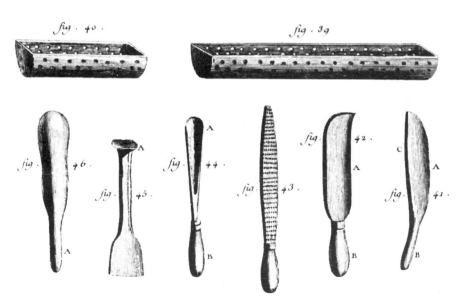

modern heating equipment to repair existing leadwork, of which three quarters is completed from reworked lead newly cast, and not less than 99.97 per cent pure. Ancient roofs that have been re-leaded include the high spire of St Mary's church, Long Sutton, Lincolnshire, Lincoln Cathedral and St Albans Cathedral.

TOOLS

Hand-crafted tools used by leadworkers today often closely resemble those illustrated in Diderot's eighteenth-century French *Encyclopaedia*. Mallets or hammers of various weights and sizes are used in conjunction with variously shaped 'bossing' tools on the surface of sheet lead. A flattening or smoothing finish may be 'fettled' with a chisel and hammer. Surfaces may be prepared for soldering or finishing with 'scrapers' which have flat heads of curved or rectangular plan set at an angle of about 45 degrees. A triangular-headed scraper will provide specific angles to fettle a shaped edge. Sheet lead for corners of roofs may be planished using mallets or blocking tools of wood. A collet or raising hammer with an oblong face similar to a mason's pickaxe is best for planishing or texturing cylindrical shapes. A convex hammer-head will dent flattened surfaces where required.

Small trowel-like tools, sometimes made specifically for a particular mould impression, are sometimes used to impress the dampened sand before it receives molten lead to produce a patterned sheet. The trowel end may be rounded or even heart-shaped. It is smaller than a builder's trowel and a steady hand is needed when impressing the sand. Templates may be required for the incision of shaped indentation channels to receive the molten lead.

A leaden font dating from about 1150, at All Saints' church, Ashover, Derbyshire, which was hidden in the rectory garden by Emmanuel Bourne during the Civil War and subsequently restored to the church by his son.

The building of Westminster Abbey, from 'The Life of Edward the Confessor' in Norman French; thirteenth century. The vertical page divider is capped with a 'châsse' reliquary, on each side of which the king is (left) receiving a gift and (right) bestowing gifts on the poor.

SMALL ARTEFACTS AND STATUARY

CROSSES

Mortuary crosses were believed to overcome the power of the devil in the grave. One was found in the tomb of an Anglo-Saxon bishop of Wells in Somerset. It was 6¼ inches (160 mm) high, bore an incised cross and was cut out of a sheet of lead. It had a thin foil of lead attached, bearing an incised memorial inscription. Another, from the monastic cemetery at Bury St Edmunds, Suffolk, inscribed CRUX CHRISTI PELLIT ('The cross of Christ drives off the enemy'), is now in the British Museum.

FONTS

In twelfth-century Britain beautiful sturdy baptismal fonts were made of lead in a style comparable to contemporary French and German fonts. About thirty have survived in England, their moulded designs still clearly discernible: cameos of farming activities and astrological symbols form borders or frames to portraits of Christian dignitaries, ceremonially robed to convey a message of goodwill.

RELIQUARIES

An early Christian reverence for the bones of saints and martyrs led to the practice of gathering their remains, sometimes consisting only of dust, into containers to be cherished in religious houses. In AD 787 church law required that all consecrated churches should possess at least one such reliquary. Leaden caskets were sometimes used for this purpose when relics were embedded in altars, church walls or even the capitals of pillars. Several examples are in the Augsburg Museum collection, at least one complete with the authenticating seal of the Bishop of Limburg.

When the translation of relics became widespread, from the eighth century AD, artists and craftsmen were commissioned to fashion works of art in metal and enamel or stonework as containers of

A silver gilt 'talking' reliquary dated about 1210 and formerly at the Cathedral Treasury, Basel. The wooden core (right) has a hollowed-out section in which to place a relic of St Eustace. (British Museum.)

lasting quality and beauty. Types included the 'châsse', a small portable gabled church-like construction, and 'talking' reliquaries, which resembled the saints' heads, hands or feet. Small pendant reliquaries made from precious metals and stones were worn as personal jewellery by wealthy Europeans by the fifteenth century. Lead was important for trial models and continued to play a significant role in the development of metal crafts.

Victorian restoration work at the church of St Mary and St Eanswyth in Folkestone, Kent, uncovered a leaden casket in the north wall. It was subsequently replaced in a chancel shrine.

PILGRIM BADGES AND TOKENS

Large numbers of leaden pilgrim badges and souvenir tokens from pilgrimage shrines have survived in Europe and many have been found in rivers or on excavated sites in England. Many originated from the shrines of Our Lady of Walsingham in Norfolk, St Edmund at Bury St Edmunds in Suffolk, or St Thomas à Becket at Canterbury, and they depict scenes from the lives of Christ and the saints. Usually the work of local craftsmen, either laymen or monks, and cheaply produced, these badges consisted of silhouettes of leaden fretwork and bore the recognised symbols for such saints as St Etheldreda, St Catherine and St Alban, besides royal saints such as Edward the Confessor or Henry VI of Windsor. Miniature leaden ampullae for holy water, oil or even dust from saints' tombs were popular purchases at shrines though leaden sporting tokens in the form of jousting knights, hawks or fish were cheerfully acquired and fastened to hats or clothing along with tokens acquired to denote place of pilgrimage. National museums have medieval carved multiple-image or two-valved moulds in stone or hardwood for mass production of leaden souvenirs. Frequently these badges were sold by the monks who made them, but others were sold by local shopkeepers. Henry VII bought 65 shillings worth for his followers and in 1481 the wife of John, Lord Howard, spent 1½d on badges and amulets for members of her household.

SEALS AND PAPAL BULLAE

Formal documents issued from the church authority in Rome became known as *bullae* when Pope Adeodatus (AD 615-18) introduced standard leaden seals to replace the wax ones previously used. When attached to papal documents concerning church organisation, appointments, ownership of land or property and church discipline, these seals were intended to establish registration authenticity and bore the Pope's name and images of St Peter and St Paul in Byzantine style. Many papacies were short-lived and frequent replacement of seal moulds was necessary.

Right: *Medieval pilgrims'
badges at Moyses Hall, Bury
St Edmunds, Suffolk: (left)
St Thomas à Becket with
archbishop's mitre, 2 by 1¼
inches (51 by 31 mm); (top
right) camel of bronze and
lead, 1⅛ by 1¾ inches (28
by 46 mm); (below right)
cameo of St Edmund or St
Sebastian of bronze and lead,
1⅜ by ¾ inch (34 by 21 mm).*

Left: *This papal seal, without
the original document, was
found at Princes Risborough,
Buckinghamshire. It bears the
name 'Martinus P.P.V.' (left)
and was issued by Pope Martin
V (1417-31). The reverse side
(right) typically depicts St Peter
and St Paul in Byzantine style
— the vibrant facial expressions
are still strikingly vivid.*

A seal attached to the original
document issued by Pope Cali-
xtus III, dated 18th April, 1458,
confirming annexation rights to
Alnesbourn Priory, Suffolk.
The silken cord is evidence of
authenticity, sealed within the
two discs of lead. The reverse
(right) shows the style of repre-
sentation of hair and beard by
specified distribution of raised
dots on the heads of the
apostles, indicating its authenticity to the original recipients.

Double-sided seals were manufactured
from two moulds as two separate artefacts and when attached to a document
were fused together to enclose a special
cord, silken for documents confirming
rights, hempen for those expressing or-
ders. It is said that the genuineness of a
papal document was apparent from the
fine dot and line details of the portraits
of the two apostles on the leaden seal or
bulla.

The use of leaden seals had become
widespread throughout Europe by the
end of the tenth century and continued
through the middle ages as a mark of
authenticity on documents certifying the
exchange of goods or the sale of property
and for similar purposes.

Portrait medal of Caterina Riva by Antonio Abondio (1538-91), an Italian medallist employed mainly by the Hapsburg courts but influenced artistically by the northern Renaissance.

MEDALS

The finely detailed draughtsmanship of engravings by, for example, Albrecht Dürer (1471-1528) was the prerequisite for the creation of portraits and miniature dramatic or heroic scenes that were cast in lead by medallists employed by rulers or church officials throughout Europe. Though much work emanated from the Roman, Florentine and Bolognese schools, outstanding examples from Germany by Friedrich Hagenauer and Christophe Weiditz in the 1520s and 1530s and from Holland by Quentin Matsys and Van Herwijck indicate a wide distribution of talent in this medium.

Medallists used a variety of processes to enhance or refine the surface of the completed leaden medal; tones of blue grey remain bright and clear on surviving Renaissance medals. Hair styles, draperies and personal characteristics provide the observer with a realistic glimpse of the style and manners of the past.

Fine line drawings continued to be produced by subsequent generations of artists, for example Annibale Caracci and pupils of the Bolognese academy. Personal and public achievements perceived to represent a new national identity began to be celebrated with specially designed medals in the seventeenth and eighteenth centuries. A century later Bertrand Andrieu portrayed Minerva in a war helmet to personify an increasingly republican French nation. In Britain Rowlandson and Cruikshank became distinguished for their fine engravings in the eighteenth and nineteenth centuries but by this time copper and brass had increased in popularity although lead continued to be used for moulds and first castings.

Right, above: A leaden jewellery model, representative of patterns used by Renaissance jewellers from about 1500 to 1630. It preceded the casting of the final product in noble metals, after which gems of the customers' choice were inserted.

Right, below: A moulded leaden boss, 2 inches (50 mm) across, possibly made in two pieces in about 1620, found in Suffolk in 1980.

16

Leaden cloth seals from bales of woven material produced at Colchester and dated to the 1570s.

JEWELLERY

As the invention of printing hastened the circulation of design pattern books throughout Europe, cheap leaden models of jewellery could be lent to customers who could choose a design and indicate their choice of materials and personal marks. These would, in turn, be interpreted by goldsmiths working with precious metals and gems. A fashion for non-religious personal jewellery, beginning in northern Italy in about 1450 with hat badges (*enseignes*), was followed a century later by a vogue for pendants to adorn ladies' necks or hair. Leaden models for these, originating chiefly from southern Germany, have survived in museum collections. They measure from about 1 inch (25 mm) long to about 3½ inches (90 mm). Designs included some Renaissance Christian motifs but classical themes were also popular.

Decorated leaden bosses for buckles or harness work were included in the jeweller's art. An example weighing 1¾

A mid nineteenth-century brooch with copper/lead silvered frame of Renaissance style, similar in outline also to some German leaden jewellery models of the early seventeenth century on display at the Historisches Museum, Basel. Height 55 mm; width 50 mm; weight 20 grams.

17

ounces (50 grams), ploughed up in a Suffolk field in 1980, has a silvery glint in its dark grey patina.

SECULAR TOKENS

Token 'money' of low denomination issued by traders or guilds for local use was in restricted circulation in England throughout the Tudor period and into the mid seventeenth century, when it was abandoned. These leaden tokens measured perhaps ¼ to ¾ inch (10-20 mm) in diameter and their designs included traders' signs, initials and dates, often interwoven with animal, floral and sun motifs, slogans or biblical texts. Some guild tokens served as membership badges.

RELIGIOUS TOKENS

Leaden tokens denoting church membership became widely adopted by nonconformist churches especially in Scotland and the north of England in the eighteenth century, though approved by John Calvin in about 1590. They had also been in use in some Anglican churches from the late Tudor period into the 1630s. Church 'token' account books for Southwark, London and Norwich parishes record the commissioning and sale of leaden communion tokens required by Easter communicants and costing one penny each. The names of parish mould-

Above: Secular and religious tokens (sixteenth century or earlier). (Top left) A secular token moulded with the initials 'TC' and with the initial 'A' on the obverse; 12 mm diameter, less than 1 mm thick; possibly early Tudor in date. (Top right) Secular token with the initial 'E', and 'B' on the obverse; 15 mm diameter, 2 mm thick; possibly late Tudor. (Bottom left) Token with the initial 'H' over 'TA' with a chalice clearly visible on the obverse; 12 mm diameter, less than 1 mm thick; possibly religious. (Bottom right) The moulded design incorporates the initial 'P' with a key and with a wheel or monastic building on the obverse, perhaps for use at the abbey, Bury St Edmunds.

Right: Some typical nineteenth-century Presbyterian church communion tokens of membership. The inscriptions on the obverse (not shown) include: 'Do this in memory of me' and 'Nec tamen consumebatur' ('That we may be spared hell's consumption').

Below: The obverse and reverse of a boy bishop token from Bury St Edmunds, inscribed in Latin with 'St Nicholas, pray for us'. Early sixteenth century.

makers and plumbers were recorded, as were the names of communicants, including Shakespearian actors in St Saviour's parish, Southwark. Purchased tokens were exchanged for communion bread and wine.

Some early leaden tokens at Moyses Hall, Bury St Edmunds, bearing religious motifs and symbols such as the crossed keys of St Petronella, the anchor of St Clement, the pomegranate or the tree of eternal life, may also have been used for attendance at religious ceremonies. In the eighteenth and nineteenth centuries individual English or Scottish nonconformist ministers commissioned wooden, stone or metal moulds for casting sacramental tokens which bore biblical inscriptions, parochial details and dates of issue or foundation. Approximately ¾ inch (20 mm) in height or diameter, they were circular, oval, octagonal or hexagonal in outline, up to 2 mm thick. Though in general use as certificates of fitness for monthly communicants, many such tokens have survived in pristine condition in museum and church treasury collections.

Tokens designed to commemorate the yearly 'election' of young boys to the honorary title of bishop during the festivals of St Nicholas or St Gregory were popular in late medieval England. Usually in the form of a leaden disc, they depicted a child wearing a mitre, holding a bishop's crozier and cross over the inscription ORA PRO NOBIS ('Pray for us').

PLAQUES

Several Anglo-Saxon leaden coffin plates have been found bearing beautifully inscribed Latin inscriptions in a style that continued in Wells for five bishoprics. Leaden memorial plaques were uncommon in England before the eighteenth century for lay people but examples survive bearing biographical details for application to coffins.

Some city parish boundaries were defined by leaden wall plaques bearing dates and badges. In Norwich, for example, St Lawrence's parish was marked by a plaque inscribed with SL, the date 1806 and a gridiron. Country estates, such as Knole in Kent, were similarly distinguished with their owner's coat of

A boundary plaque from Knole, Kent, bearing the Sackville crest.

arms, to match existing leaden pipes, sockets, strapwork or cisterns.

Though the exquisitely beautiful plaques and plaquettes produced by Peter Flotner (1485-1546) depicting Old Testament themes such as Anger, Justice, Mystery and Belief or human follies and aspirations have had few rivals to their perfection, a revived practical interest has been evident in England in the 1970s and 1980s.

STATUARY

By the eighteenth century ways of reinforcing lead for intricate statuary became widely understood. A process of 'hammering' sheet lead by hand produced a fine-grained structural texture on the surface, less liable to corrode. New recipes to induce patina formation were evolved, some even imitating the appearance of bronze or marble.

The creation of larger-than-life statues, often designed as groups with a theme, became fashionable and they were com-

'Shepherd boy' decorative wall plaque from Lavenham, Suffolk, dated 1985. The mould was carved and the plaque cast by a local artist.

missioned for landscaped gardens in imitation of those at Versailles. William III and Mary II favoured the Dutch garden style, the perfect medium for displaying lead sculpture by artists such as Jan van Nost, who set up his workshop in Piccadilly, London. His output was prodigious and created a continuing demand. Van Nost's groups of leaden putti and his massive 'Four Seasons' urn at Melbourne Hall, Derbyshire, are master-

pieces of this medium. John Cheere purchased van Nost's moulds and the contents of his studio, but as few eighteenth-century leaden statues bore the artist's name it is difficult to assign authorship to extant examples. Nine leaden life-sized 'character' figures at Wallington, Northumberland, are thought to be van Nost's work. The equestrian statue of William III at Petersfield, Hampshire, and a life-sized figure of George II dress-

Strapwork on leaden pipes with the initials 'TD' for Thomas, Earl of Dorset.

Left: *An eighteenth-century statue of Charity, possibly from the van Nost studio, restored and repainted by English Heritage. It stands on its original plinth in the front garden of the Fishermen's Hospital, Great Yarmouth.*

Right: *After centuries of weathering, this cast leaden urn entitled 'Four Seasons' by Jan van Nost, at Melbourne Hall, Derbyshire, remains an impressively intricate example of ingenious metal casting and lead sculpting. It dates from about 1720.*

ed as a Roman warrior at the Royal Citadel, Plymouth, are from the same era of English outdoor sculpture.

Lead sculptors like van Nost and John Cheere created humorous statues for the gardens of the rich, as well as more obviously serious works. Plump putti were designed to peep mischievously from grottoes or lawns; garden urns became larger and increasingly complex sculptures, designed both to interest and to entertain the observer.

21

This fluted filigree horizontal rainhead at Knole, Kent, is similar to an Elizabethan example at St John's College, Cambridge.

RAINHEADS

Towards the end of the fifteenth century red brick was becoming fashionable for fine houses in England and the Netherlands, and sheet lead was used to make stylish 'heads' to disperse rainwater from roofs into downpipes, in preference to stone gargoyles. The cost of lead extraction in England was increasing as deeper veins had to be exploited and only the rich could afford to use lead in buildings. For Westminster Palace 'square pipes of leade, garnyshid with the kinges armes and badges' were ordered. By the end of the sixteenth century large town or country houses could support rainheads or 'hoppers', sometimes 5 feet (1.5 metres) long, to receive the rain, often from lead-clad roofs, and to disperse it into pipes to feed cisterns at ground or other levels. Hammered, twisted and cut to intricate designs, perhaps painted and gilded, rainheads began to assume the visual design characteristics of contemporary art forms. Outstanding examples can be seen at Haddon Hall, Derbyshire, Knole House, Kent, and St John's College, Oxford.

Hampton Court Palace, Middlesex, was converted for use as an official residence by Cardinal Wolsey in the 1520s. The high red-brick walls, bonded in intricate geometric designs and pierced by tall leaded windows, required long narrow lightweight downpipes with leaden clips to support them. The intricate roof angles required rainheads moulded to a shape which would coax away accumulated rainfall. King Henry VIII's subsequent ownership is evidenced by the Tudor rose, portcullis and Lorraine-style initials on rainheads and sockets. Further rainheads and downpipes moulded with the initials of later monarchs have been added to existing or new wings.

In the seventeenth and eighteenth centuries the Sackville family undertook considerable improvements and extensions to Knole, their house in Kent. One range

A new wing added to Hampton Court Palace by Sir Christopher Wren for William III and Mary II, with lion-head rainheads to match classical stone-work of the late seventeenth century.

is fitted with moulded leadwork which clearly reflects a plainer style of rainhead that was in vogue in the 1630s in the Netherlands, where the Earl of Dorset, a Sackville, was ambassador. By 1658 the Knole accounts record payments of £200 per year to a plumber, Jerome Read, for work at Knole House and Dorsett House. By the mid eighteenth century some of the estate's leadwork 'wanted new casting' and pipes had to be drained in frosty weather. Valuable windows were being damaged by dispersed rainwater though much was channelled out through the pierced filigree leadwork of the rainheads if they became overloaded.

In the University of Oxford, rainheads of the seventeenth and eighteenth centuries at St John's and Trinity colleges are representative of the best leadwork in vogue at the time of installation. Archbishop Laud provided funds to add a new range of buildings and quadrangle to St John's College in 1630. Old leadwork had to be reinstated and new crested rainheads installed as it was here that the King and Queen were to be entertained on its completion. No effort was spared and John Lufton, fellow and scholar of the college, was entrusted with finding the best materials and engaging the most adept craftsmen for the proposed leadwork, records of which he entered in the college account book. The painting of the massive rainheads or 'cisterns' and pipes was recorded in this way and they

Crested, battlemented, linen-folded rainhead with filigree perforations, the applied colour or tinning just visible, still functional and aesthetically pleasing; at Knole, Kent.

Centrally placed over the downpipe, this rainhead is designed to control the collection of surging rainwater from the roof at Knole and is one of a series around the outside of the house.

Above: *This late seventeenth-century moulded rainhead on the Bodleian Library, Oxford University, is flanked by ornamental stone winged beasts which themselves could deflect splashes of rain from window casings.*

Above right: *A moulded cleat fastening on a downpipe on the Bodleian Library, with initials perhaps of Thomas Bodley.*

Below right: *One of the two cisterns dated 1635 at St John's College, Oxford, bearing the arms of Archbishop Laud of Canterbury. It matches a similar rainhead with Charles I's arms on it. They adorn the new Laud range and quadrangle built to mark the King's official visit.*

can still be seen displaying the arms of Charles I and Archbishop Laud. At Trinity College the arms of Bathurst, the college's President, appear on the face of one rainhead on the chapel built by him in the 1690s.

Also in Oxford, some moulded, initialled, early seventeenth-century leadwork remains on the Bodleian Library, which has undergone a number of architectural changes since its foundation, and flamboyantly ornate rainheads are a noticeable feature of the New Examination Schools of 1878-82, designed by Sir Thomas Jackson.

York rainheads: (top left) a dated Elizabethan rainhead, practical and unobtrusive; (top centre) a personalised rainhead for an eighteenth-century city house, 24 St Savioursgate; (top right) an elegant design of crossed arrows above a patterned flute, at 77 Bootham; (bottom left) a well balanced architectural 'hopper' with classical motifs applied; (bottom centre) a simple rounded rainhead with a mascot-like elephant above; (bottom right) classical motifs applied to rainhead and matching angular downpipe in Castlegate.

Left: *A rainhead at Kentwell Hall, Long Melford, Suffolk, bearing the Clopton family arms. A Clopton will in 1541 referred to the 'ledes and brasse' at Long Melford.*

Right: *A seventeenth-century rainhead, moulded with the cockatrice crest of the Cordell family, founders of Melford Hall, an Elizabethan house at Long Melford, where subsequent leadwork dates from the sixteenth to nineteenth centuries.*

Audley End House, Essex, built as a palace for Thomas, Earl of Suffolk, in about 1606, although much restored, has some original characteristic seventeenth-century leaden rainheads, one bearing the date 1686 and James II's initials, another those of William III and Mary II, dated 1689. Great quantities of reused lead cover the roof today.

In Georgian times York became the fashionable and social centre for north-eastern England, and the Mansion House, a theatre and many fine brick houses were built by the city merchants and prominent landowners, while some existing medieval and late Tudor houses received Georgian facades. One successful physician distinguished his house in 1720 with a statue of the Roman god of healing over the front door. Surviving leaden rainheads and accompanying leadwork in York represent high standards of craftsmanship; artistic details have strength and symmetry and embody neatly balanced basket-weave designs, floral and animal motifs.

A rare early seventeenth-century circular cistern with the Lewis family crest, mounted on a plinth near its original site at St Fagans Castle, South Glamorgan.

ORNATE CISTERNS

Several hundred leaden water cisterns moulded with geometric designs or designs embodying real and imaginary flora and fauna have survived in England and Wales. The earliest, dated 1612, is at the Middle Temple, London. It was last used as a drinks cooler, lined with zinc to exclude heat and fitted with an oak lid. An account of its unusual history is inscribed in Gothic-style red, blue and gold script on a copper strip countersunk into the edge of the lid.

The majority of these leaden cisterns are of eighteenth-century origin, the heyday of this kind of leadwork in England. Though mention of leaden cisterns in records and inventories indicates their use in medieval and Tudor times, none has survived from those periods. Some had been set more than 6 feet (2 metres) below ground to escape the effects of frost; alternative water supplies sometimes came from pits simply lined with clay and lime as at Wandlebury, Cam-

bridgeshire, or from cisterns in the ground constructed from logs, like the one discovered in medieval Oyster Street, Portsmouth.

The leaden sheets for cistern construction were made by pouring molten lead into a hard-packed dampened sand-bed already impressed with carved moulds. The sheets were bent into shape and soldered to a base. This method of providing decorative but durable tubs cheaply remained unchallenged until the nineteenth century. There are several French leaden tubs of the twelfth and thirteenth centuries, circular or oval in plan, in London museums. Their storage capacity is generally smaller than that of English cisterns though several have original taps. Animals and plants, sometimes with fleurs-de-lis interspersed, form friezes of decoration around these diminutive tanks. An early twelfth-century cylindrical example from France bears a cartouche enclosing the Virgin and Child

Right: *A typical early Georgian water-storage cistern with mythical, semi-mythical and natural creatures within a stengthening all-over grid pattern in which St George rides confidently, shield on arm. (Museum of London.)*

Below: *Close-up of a panel from a cistern moulded with the Spring family coat of arms and the initials of Sir Thomas Spring and his wife Merilina (1703). (Moyses Hall, Bury St Edmunds.)*

This deep cistern was brought from a London garden in 1925 to become a permanent flower container at Anglesey Abbey, Cambridgeshire. The equine sculpture was added as part of Lord Fairhaven's garden design.

with St John the Baptist between two cherubs' heads. The additional bands of hunting scenes and vases with floral scrolls need not have precluded its use for liturgical purposes when required.

For large town and country houses in England from the sixteenth to the mid nineteenth century, leaden cisterns stored water off the roofs. Sometimes, at roof-top level, they fed bathroom tanks or, at kitchen level, they acted as sinks perhaps in association with indoor wells and pumps. Various decorative features served also to protect the lead surface from inadvertent blows and denting. Outside, rainwater cisterns provided a water supply in case of fire and for filling watering cans. By about 1900 urban water-supply schemes and mass-produced galvanised water tanks had replaced leaden cisterns, which were already valued as antiques.

The London cisterns in particular were frequently moulded with an impressive variety of the stylised or natural flower heads popularised by botanical artists employed by French and German courts. Walter Gedde's pattern book, *A Book of Sundry Draughtes* (1615), had already provided the angular interlacing and framework for these designs, leaving lit-

tle space for legends. One surviving example, however, given to the Victoria and Albert Museum, bears the following inscription: ST MARY'S WHITECHAPEL — JOHN HINTON — CHURCHWARDEN — 1721.

A handsome panelled cistern with the date 1709, marked with a double rose, shell and ducal crown at Marlborough House, near St James's Palace, London, seems likely to be that referred to by Sir Christopher Wren in his building reports to the Duchess of Marlborough, for whom he acted as architect.

When John and Catherine Gurney set up home in 1777 in Norwich they opened a bank in their parlour. They commissioned a cistern with their initials moulded below the date of their marriage and entwined with a love knot and garlands of flowers. Now covered with a grey-green patina, the cistern stands in the grounds of the Walsingham Abbey estate, the present home of the Gurney family.

Semicircular or octagonal cisterns are rare survivals in twentieth-century England and Wales. There is a small semicircular one at Carreglwyd, Anglesey, moulded with the date 1763 and the initials IM over G for John and Mary Griffiths.

30

FURTHER READING

Blomfield, R. T. *Renaissance Architecture in England 1500-1800*. G. Bell and Sons, 1900.
Gotch, J. A. *The English Home, Charles I to George IV*. B. T. Batsford, 1918.
Hackenbroch, Yvonne. *Renaissance Jewellery*. Sotheby Parke Bernet, 1979.
Irving, Richard. *Metalwork Step by Step*. Frederick Warne, 1961.
Magne, Lucien. *L'Art Appliqué aux Métiers: Décor du Métal*, volume 6. Paris, 1922.
Michiner, M. *Medieval Pilgrim and Secular Badges*. Hawkins Publications, 1986.
Morgan, E. G. 'The Ancient Craft of Cast Lead: Roman to Nineteenth Century', *Foundry Trade Journal*, 153 (September 1982), 3246.
Murray, Peter and Linda. *A Dictionary of Art and Artists*. Penguin, 1971.
Neuhaus, August. 'Blei', *Reallexicon zur Deutschen Kunstgeschichte*, II, 874-83. Stuttgart, 1948.
Petrie, Sir William Flinders. *Arts and Crafts in Ancient Egypt*. P. N. Foulis, 1910.
Rickard, Thomas Arthur. *Man and Metals*. McGraw-Hill, 1932.
Serafini, Camillo. *Le Monete e Le Bolle* ('Coins and Seals'). Rome, 1910-28.
Sutton-Goold, P. M. 'Antique Lead Cisterns', *Antique Collecting*, 20 (1985), 4.
Toynbee, J. M. C. *The Art of the Romans*. Thames and Hudson, 1965.
Tylecote, R. F. *A History of Metallurgy*. Metals Society, London, 1976.
Wood, Eric S. *Archaeology*. Collins Field Guides, 1973.

PLACES TO VISIT

Examples of historic leadwork can be seen at these museums. Intending visitors are advised to find out opening times before making a special journey.

MUSEUMS IN GREAT BRITAIN
Ashmolean Museum of Art and Archaeology, Beaumont Street, Oxford OX1 2PH. Telephone: 0865 278000.
Bridewell Museum of Norwich Trades and Industries, Bridewell Alley, Norwich, Norfolk NR2 1AQ. Telephone: 0603 667228.
The British Museum, Great Russell Street, London WC1B 3DG. Telephone: 071-636 1555.
Colchester and Essex Museum, The Castle, Colchester, Essex CO1 1TJ. Telephone: 0206 712490.
Derby Central Museum and Art Gallery, The Strand, Derby DE1 1BS. Telephone: 0332 293111 extension 782.
Fitzwilliam Museum, Trumpington Street, Cambridge CB2 1RB. Telephone: 0223 332900.
Moyses Hall, Cornhill, Bury St Edmunds, Suffolk IP33 1DX. Telephone: 0284 763233 extensions 7488 and 7489.
Museum of London, London Wall, London EC2Y 5HN. Telephone: 071-600 3699.
Reading Museum and Art Gallery, Blagrave Street, Reading, Berkshire RG1 1QH. Telephone: 0734 399809.
Victoria and Albert Museum, Cromwell Road, South Kensington, London SW7 2RL. Telephone: 071-938 8500.
Weald and Downland Open Air Museum, Singleton, Chichester, West Sussex PO18 0EU. Telephone: 024363 348.

MUSEUMS IN OTHER COUNTRIES
Historisches Museum Basel, Barfüsserkirche, 4052 Basel, Switzerland.
Musée de Cluny, 6 Place Paul-Painlevé, 75005 Paris, France.
Osterreichische Galerie, Schloss Belvedere, Prinz-Eugenstrasse 27, 1030 Vienna 3, Austria.

OTHER PLACES

These are some of the places in Britain where decorative leadwork may be seen *in situ* on buildings or as statuary in gardens, etcetera.

Anglesey Abbey, Cambridgeshire (cistern).
Ashover, Derbyshire: All Saints' church (font).
Audley End House, Essex (rainheads).
Blickling Hall, Norfolk (rainheads).
Cambridge: Selwyn College (roof of new building); Emmanuel, Pembroke, St John's and Trinity Colleges (rainheads).
Carreglwyd, Anglesey, Gwynedd (cistern).
Chelsea, London: Royal Hospital (cisterns).
Finchingfield, Essex: Spains Hall (rainheads).
Great Yarmouth, Norfolk: Fishermen's Hospital (statue of Charity).
Guildford, Surrey: Hospital of Blessed Trinity (rainheads).
Haddon Hall, Derbyshire (rainheads).
Hampton Court Palace, Middlesex (rainheads).
Kimbolton Castle, Cambridgeshire (rainheads).
Knole, Kent (rainheads and cisterns).
Leighton Bromswold, Cambridgeshire: St Mary's church (rainheads).
Leominster, Herefordshire: Priory Church of St Peter and St Paul (rainheads).
Lincoln: cathedral (roof).
London: City halls of Girdlers, Innholders, Merchant Taylors and some other livery companies (cisterns).
Long Melford, Suffolk: Holy Trinity church (window roundel); Kentwell Hall and Melford Hall (rainheads).
Long Sutton, Lincolnshire: St Mary's church (leaded spire).
Lower Halstow, Kent: St Margaret's church (font).
Melbourne Hall, Derbyshire (garden sculpture).
North Marston, Buckinghamshire: church (roof leadwork).
Norwich, Norfolk: St John's Roman Catholic cathedral (pierced leadwork on the roof); Steward House (rainheads).
Oxford: Bodleian Library, New Examination Schools, St John's College and Trinity college (rainheads).
Petersfield, Hampshire (statue of William III).
Plush Manor, Dorset (cistern).
Plymouth, Devon: Royal Citadel (statue of George II).
Poundisford Park, Pitminster, Taunton, Somerset (water butt).
Rainham Hall, Essex (rainheads).
St Albans, Hertfordshire: cathedral (roof).
St Fagans Castle, South Glamorgan (cistern).
Sherborne, Dorset: Old School House (roof leadwork).
Shipley, West Yorkshire: Inland Revenue Accounts Office, Welfare Block (multi-faceted roof with nineteen pyramids).
Wallington, Northumberland (statues).
York: houses in St Savioursgate, Bootham and Castlegate (rainheads).